Online Relationships to Military

LONG
DISTANCE
RELATIONSHIPS

BEN JACKSON & SAM LAWRENCE

Disclaimer

All attempts have been made to verify the information contained in this book but the author and publisher do not bear any responsibility for errors or omissions. Any perceived negative connotation of any individual, group, or company is purely unintentional. Furthermore, this book is intended as entertainment only and as such, any and all responsibility for actions taken upon reading this book lies with the reader alone and not with the author or publisher. This book is not intended as medical, legal, or business advice and the reader alone holds sole responsibility for any consequences of any actions taken after reading this book. Additionally, it is the reader's responsibility alone and not the author's or publisher's to ensure that all applicable laws and regulations for business practice are adhered to.

To all the couples out there who struggle daily being apart from your your partner. Just remember if they are the one it's so worth the fight. Don't give up.

.

CONTENTS

INTRODUCTION

A S AN INTRODUCTION to this book, we decided to tell you a little bit more about who we are and why we have decided to write this. Ben and I have been together for just over two years now, but have known each other for about three years altogether. This will give you an idea of who we are, how we met and how we have progressed from complete strangers to a happily married couple in around three years.

We met online playing a game that we both downloaded to our iPhones. Imagine that! A free game that cost us nothing to download led to the romance and eventual marriage of two strangers. The game involved fighting against other players in real-time strategy, building up our characters and joining forces to fight as a team. We started off just as friends fighting on different sides and quickly turned into the best of friends. Eventually we teamed up to fight alongside each other and soon started to spend more and more time talking and chatting.

I was going through a separation with my husband during this time and the game was a way for me to get some time to myself. It also gave me something that I could do where I didn't have to worry about all of my concerns at home. Ben was someone who gave me advice and truth when I needed it. Our communication back then first revolved around the chat function that was built into the game. Then we moved onto texts through a messaging app called Touch. After the messaging we moved onto our first voice-to-voice chatting, using Voxer. This allowed us to leave voice messages for each other, much like an online walkie-talkie. After the texting and voice messages we soon moved onto calling each other. At first I bought calling cards, but after you have been on the phone five or six hours they soon became too expensive. Next we tried chatting through apps that just used data instead of traditional phone calls; data is a lot cheaper than international phone calls! We discovered that our feelings had turned into more than just friends when jealously started to creep into our friendship.

We took the plunge into a long-distance relationship in February with no real first meeting date in sight. The reason for this was that our jobs and money wouldn't allow for it. We both worked positions that didn't allow us to simply drop things and rush off. Oh, how different things would have been if we were rich millionaires. I got the chance of a lifetime to arrange a quick two-week trip in April. We quickly organized everything to the best of our abilities and seven weeks later I arrived in Brisbane, Australia for the first time. Fifty hours of flying, three plane rides, one missed flight and a twenty-four-hour layover later, I arrived. Fresh as a daisy, hardly, but still nervous and more excited than I had ever been in my entire life. For anyone that has been through this first meeting before, you will know the butterflies are floating around inside your stomach like crazy.

I landed and felt like I was going to get sick, especially when they decided to scan my bag again at immigration. Talk about making me nervous! I knew Ben was just as nervous as me and now I was waiting while some customs guys looked through my panties. When I walked through those doors I saw Ben standing there with flowers and the biggest goofy grin on his face that I had ever seen. We hugged awkwardly with a quick kiss, but the giant smiles plastered across our faces told the whole story. We held hands while we walked through the airport towards the rental car company's desk to pick up our car. This is when Ben kissed me properly for the first time.

I was floating on air and it's true that my toes curled up a little bit because of the electricity of this first kiss. After all this time it was surreal to be standing there with him and able to touch his skin, taste his lips and smell him for the first time ever. We spent two weeks together the first time that we met. We hired a small cottage and it was the best holiday that either of us had, and as holidays go it went far too quickly. The first time that we met we both expected there to be a certain amount of nerves. It's always awkward when you meet people for the first time, friends, family and dates especially. When you meet someone for a date for the first time, there is always that feeling like you're going to throw up or pass out, unless you're a dating expert that is! Well, we had none of that, no nerves - it was like we had known each other for years.

It's a strange feeling to be with someone who you've never met, and to be instantly comfortable with that person. We laughed, we cried, we argued, we had fun and most of all, we had each other for the first time ever. It's a hard feeling to describe to someone who hasn't gone through it before, that feeling of meeting your soul mate for the first time. Imagine how it feels when your loved one returns from a long trip, but that trip has been forever. It's sort of like that, multiplied by a thousand.

After that magical two weeks ended, it was a quick trip down the slide, back to reality. Now we had confirmed something that up until then had only been a feeling: we were meant to be together, forever. In the next seven weeks Sam organized to attend a course in Australia and we both moved in with each other for five months. The sacrifice that she made in uprooting her life, arranging for the care of her children with their father and her mother, and moving to another country are priceless. I will never be able to repay her for this initial sacrifice on her part; that five months were what we needed as a couple, to cement our relationship, forever.

Ever since then our relationship has consisted of approximately 3 to 4 week visits, at the most. The breaks between visits is normally about 8 weeks but can last all the way up to 14 weeks if the schedule works out that way. We try to book our visits when tickets are cheap and we are becoming quite good at picking the airlines' schedules! Most of our visits correspond with special events and holidays when we can, like anniversaries, birthdays etc.

We have recently gotten married and started our immigration process, which is another nightmare all together, but with patience and time we are hoping to successfully navigate it.

Our story isn't over; it's only just begun.

We hope that you enjoy our story and our book.

Thanks

Ben & Sam.

CHAPTER ONE
WHAT IS A LONG-DISTANCE RELATIONSHIP?

WHAT IS A long-distance relationship? Good question, and it has a very simple definition too. Oxford Dictionaries defines a long-distance relationship as:

Sounds simple, right? Wrong. It's just three simple words, that when combined add up to a logistical nightmare that destroys all but the strongest relationships. They say that relationships that go through an ordeal are stronger for it; well, long-distance relationships are an ordeal that lasts from the beginning of the relationship, until it ends or the distance is bridged.

Having been in a long-term, long-distance relationship now for almost three years, I'm struggling to find anything else that would test a relationship as much. Sudden traumatic events like a death or accident are certainly traumatic. That is one problem that could result in either long-term or short-term problems in a relationship. Illnesses that last a particularly long time could be something similar to the effects that distance can have on a relationship.

It's hard to explain to someone who hasn't been in a long-distance relationship how hard it can actually be on a relationship. When you have a fight, you just can't kiss and make up. When you're upset you can't just give your partner a hug to cheer them up. When you laugh together it's over the phone or through a text message. When you share your good news, you can't look into your partner's eyes and see how happy they are for you. When you need a shoulder to cry on, there isn't a shoulder there to cry on.

Technology becomes your new best friend when you are in a long-distance relationship, and money can be your worst enemy. Your cellphone, laptop, iPad or tablet become attached to you as if they were handcuffed to your arm. It's funny how we check to make sure we have our mobile phones before we check whether we have our wallet or car keys. From personal experience, when my phone either stops working or I misplace it, panic sets in pretty damn quick. Even if Sam is asleep, I still like to know that if she wakes up, I'll be there to answer her message or call, if she needs me.

We don't have a lot of money between us. We both work hard and save to be able to travel between our two countries and visit each other. Mine and Sam's countries couldn't really be much further apart if we tried; we definitely aren't an hour's drive apart. As a rough guide, it's normally a minimum of 3 flights, and 40 hours traveling time for us just to hold hands. Not to mention the fact that the return flight can run anywhere from as cheap as $1600 right through to $3000. Would it be easier if we were rich? Damn right, I imagine it would be a lot easier to travel without having to worry about money. Unfortunately we aren't filthy rich; we aren't even well off, and we barely make enough to cover life's expenses let alone travel. Would I take the cash instead of the relationship? I wouldn't swap it for anything and neither would Sam.

So if you are in any sort of long-distance relationship, you'll have hardships to overcome. Some may be harder than others - distance, money, time, children - but they all have things that you'll need to overcome. No long-distance relationship is easy and some are just downright almost impossible. How you overcome the problems in your relationship is how it will be defined. You can give up on the problems that you face, label them too hard and then move on. Or you could work to overcome the problems that you face together. You and your partner can work together and build on the strengths that you gain from overcoming the obstacles that you face in a long-distance relationship.

Our long-distance relationship is on the extreme end of the long-distance scale. Other people's relationships might only be hours away, while some might only be in the next town. There are other factors that normally force people to continue in long-distance relationships. Separate states would be hard because of the distance, but if you're in the same country then you have a big advantage. Some people start off in a normal relationship but then it evolves into a long-distance relationship. This could be because of family, friends or work.

People take jobs where they often travel because of work; they could move, do fly-in fly-out work or drive-in and drive-out work. People in the military often have to deal with their partner being away from home for extended periods. Not only are they in a long-distance relationship that is extremely stressful, but they also have to deal with the fact that their loved one could be in a lot of danger. Most people know what their partners are doing generally - at work, at the gym, out for dinner or maybe at a game. When your partner is overseas on deployment, you don't know what it is they're doing a lot of the time. This adds another layer of stress to an already stressful situation.

There isn't an easy, one-size-fits-all approach to any long-distance relationship. No long-distance relationship is going to be exactly the same as another, nor will they face the same problems and hardships. How you handle the situations that you face in your long-distance relationship will define the outcome, good or bad.

CHAPTER TWO

COMMUNICATION, TOOLS, TRICKS AND TIPS

W E LIVE IN a modern age where technology is advancing faster than we can keep track of. Therefore, taking advantage of everything available is extremely important. This isn't fifty years ago where it took weeks to travel, and we have different ways of communicating other than mail. Email, phone calls, instant messages and apps for making calls are all cheap and instant ways of staying in touch with our loved ones. We take advantage of every possible way that we can to stay in touch, the cheaper the better. Sometimes the cheapest ways aren't the best though, so you have to find a balance. It's no use having the cheapest phone plan if you don't get coverage, or when you do it's patchy and you can't hear the other person speaking.

We are will cover a few different things in this chapter. The advantages of different mobile phone plans and what you should be looking for. Different apps that you can use for iPhone or Android operating systems. Cheap phone cards that you can load onto your mobile. Different ways in which you can write to each other like instant messages and emails. There are heaps of different things out there, and most are free. Just seeing someone type the words at the end of a hard day, before you sleep, can take some of the loneliness away.

Technology is great; believe me, we couldn't do what we do without it. But don't forget about the traditional ways either. Taking the time to sit down and write someone a letter, on paper, is a great feeling. It's hard to explain the feeling when you receive a package, or a letter from a loved one. Something physical to touch, to smell, is a major thing in a relationship. It might not always be practical to only talk using this way, but sometimes it's nice to surprise someone who you love. You might also surprise yourself while you're writing it. Sometimes it's nice and therapeutic to write down how we feel, and maybe you will be a little better off because of it.

Don't just take our word for it though. Most of these apps are free, and are also available for both iOS and Android phones. Some of them you have most likely already been using. We're just going to list a few of the more popular ones for you without turning this entire thing into a technology report.

First off is one that most people are familiar with, Facebook. You can keep in contact, send messages and if you download its partner Facebook Messenger then you can call and message people without adding them to your Facebook friends list. Facebook and Facebook Messenger are both free to use and free to download.

Next is an old classic that most people have used before. What you probably don't know is that if you upgrade your Skype then you can use it to call any mobile numbers. So it's free just to call your Skype friends, or you can pay a little extra for credits and call overseas number or mobiles. Skype was one of the pioneers of chatting and video calling, but now you can carry it with you.

One of the most popular apps out there for both iPhone and Android phones is WhatsApp. Chances are, everyone has this app or has had it at some point in the past. You can create groups, send messages, pictures, videos and also audio files. You can't call someone directly with WhatsApp, but you can record audio messages and send them. WhatsApp is free for the first year and only $1 US per year after that.

This is one app that both Sam and I use every day when we are apart, and so do over 516 million other users world-wide. You can set it so it searches through your phone's contacts and tells you who is already using Viber. It allows you to send instant messages, videos, audio, and you can call directly with Viber too. It's free to download and use, and available for both Android and iOS devices. You can also call other users using Viber's new video chat function.

Another app that we use and find very fun is the Line app. We found this one day when we were both getting angry at our calls dropping out and thought it might be the app we were using. Turns out it wasn't but still, we had another app to use. Same as Viber, but with a lot more fun stickers and better for creating groups of people. Line allows people on iOS and Android phones to hang out easily and chat. Free to use and download, and a good fun app. Line also has a video chat function.

Another classic app that has been around for a while is KiK. Same features as the other apps with a small feature that's kind of cool. You can use a browser in the app to settle any arguments that you might have, or just to show whoever you're chatting with something. Free to use and download.

The last one I'm going to write about is Voxer. This is good for messages and voice messages, but you can't call off Voxer. I'm mentioning it here specifically because we used it during the early stages of our relationship. Free to download and free to use, and available on both iOS and Android devices.

So there are some great apps that you can use to easily speak with your loved one if they have access to the internet or Wi-Fi. When you're traveling you might not have a mobile plan in that particular country, which can make it harder. However, free Wi-Fi is becoming more and more popular these days, with parks, businesses and even entire towns offering free Wi-Fi to attract more business.

If you are just going to be in one particular country then it could be wise to consider getting a prepaid account to use there. When I am traveling through the United States I switch out my SIM card and replace it with one for use in the United States. I log online before I leave Australia and load it up with $5 credit for the days that I will be traveling. I specifically switched from a mobile phone plan to buying a phone outright that was unlocked. This would allow me to switch SIMs easily, no matter which country I am in at the time.

Another option for when you're traveling overseas is to just buy a cheap prepaid phone. If you're in that country long enough to make it worthwhile, it's definitely a good idea. Overseas roaming charges can be an expensive way to learn what not to do, so be careful. Depending on how long you talk, and whether you make audio or video calls, you will definitely use some data. So be aware of the fact that regardless of whether you are using your phone at home or abroad, your data can get used up pretty quickly.

We didn't use phone cards for very long in our relationship, as they were a pretty expensive option. You could purchase the cards and then recharge them online. There were different options that were hard to navigate sometimes too. For example you could talk longer and it would be cheaper, or shorter and cheaper, but if you talked too long or not long enough then you got charged for it. I wouldn't personally recommend them unless it was for a one-off or emergency type situations. They also had a horrible connection compared to the data connections.

If you and your partner both have iPhones or iPads then you can take advantage of the iMessage and FaceTime features. You can't just call up your partner if they have an Android phone and you have an iPhone, but there are definitely some easy ways around the problem. Viber, Line and Skype are all free and they all have the ability to video chat. The only thing that you're missing is the integration that iPhone users enjoy with FaceTime. It's built into the phone's system, which makes calling a lot easier and users don't have to log in or download anything.

Don't forget the old-fashioned ways of staying in contact either. You can send mail and packages to each other to add a little romance to the relationship, although it's not exactly state of the art and won't help you much if there is an emergency!

Email is another often overlooked way through which couples can stay in contact with each other. It's also easier to keep track of conversations when you have an email record of them. Nowadays we mostly use email for business, not our personal life. If you don't have a great internet connection, then emails could be the answer you're looking for.

They say communication is the key to maintaining a good relationship. It's no different in a long-distance relationship; if anything, it's twice as important. You have to be able to maintain that link with your partner as much as possible. You don't have the chance to simply go home after work, kiss and make up. As such, being able to call and text as much as possible is extremely important. Sam and I normally speak on my lunch break, every day while I'm at work and before work. After I finish work she is sleeping so we don't get a chance to speak then. I like to stay up as late as I can, as this way I can say good morning to her when she wakes up for work.

On a weekend we get to hang out more and chat a bit. It isn't unusual to see either one of us walking around, playing with our kids, shopping or even working out. The only difference is that we have a headset hanging out of our ears. It's become quite normal for both of us to go on with our normal day-to-day lives, but chat to each other as we go. This is one way that we can stay in touch and maintain some contact in our relationship. We try to FaceTime each other on a weekend when we can and also we constantly message each other, just like a normal couple would.

Our situation is pretty drastic though, and not like most people's. Due to the fact that we live on opposite sides of the world, our time zones are pretty much the opposite. If you and your partner are in different states then your time zones might only be hours apart. This makes it a lot easier to talk, but still doesn't make the situation any easier. No long-distance relationship is easy - hours, minutes, days apart, it's all hard.

CHAPTER THREE
MILITARY LIFE & FIFO
WORK (FLY IN FLY OUT)

LONG-DISTANCE RELATIONSHIPS CAN be hard enough for both partners, but when you add military service and deployment into the mix, it's an entirely different ball game. Even the strongest relationship can be strained because of long distance, and that isn't taking into consideration the added stress of the fear of injury or death. Any sort of military life is full of hardships; there is a lot of moving, and many other stressful factors that can cause relationships to fail. That doesn't mean it's all bad; there are also many great things about military life, and many people consider themselves better off for it.

Another form of this type of long-distance relationship is Fly In Fly Out work, or FIFO. There isn't always the amount of danger that's associated with a partner being away on a military deployment, and normally the time frame is shorter, but they are equally as hard. Your loved one is away from you, normally anywhere from one week, to eight weeks, and sometimes longer. The money is often the reason for this, as sometimes a lack of work close to home leads people away. The resulting stresses on the relationship are the same: separation, fear and loneliness.

There are some great ways that can help you to prepare and deal with being away from a loved one. Remember, whatever you're feeling, if you are the person who is away or at home, your partner is most likely feeling very similar things to you. Don't ever be afraid to reach out and let someone know if you're feeling depressed. Depression can be quite common in people working away from their home, and the people left behind. This can be particularly hard on young couples, or couples that haven't spent a lot of time apart from one another.

Planning ahead can be a key factor in making sure that everyone is prepared for the separation, both mentally and physically. The roles of people will most likely change during this period; one partner will have to assume the roles of the person who is away. Things that come up during the day - a crisis, challenges or problems that would normally involve both people - must now be handled alone. You always have to remember that even though it may be hard alone at home, it can be equally hard on the person who is away. They may be aware of the problems that you're dealing with alone, but feel helpless so far away, not being able to help you. As much planning as possible will help you both face any challenges that may arise. The more you plan, the more prepared you both will be. Below are a few important things to remember:

- Create family rosters and plan your weeks/days.

- Prepare all your finances as much as possible. Try and be aware of any upcoming bills, or maintenance that will have to be taken care of.

- Plan for any emergencies. Have a list of friends and family that you can turn to.

- Prepare and discuss how you will stay in contact with one another: email, text, messages, phone calls, faxes or video calls.

- Try to organize as much as possible when you will stay in

contact. This can be very important for children, who by nature are particular about routines.

- Prepare a network of support: friends, family, workmates or professional help.

- Make sure that you stay as busy as possible. Just because one partner is away, it doesn't mean that the other person should sit at home alone. Take part in local community activities, play a sport, start a hobby or visit friends and family.

Trust while apart is often a major part of long-distance relationships. We aren't going to go too much into it in this chapter because we will be covering it in more detail throughout the book. If a relationship is shaky before a separation or one partner doesn't trust the other, then it will quite often fail during the separation. You must learn to trust that your partner will make the right decisions while they are either at home or away.

It doesn't matter if a relationship is long distance, FIFO, military or just a normal relationship, respect is extremely important. If one partner doesn't respect the other it can lead to a breakdown in communication and trust. Make sure that you talk about this with each other. Establish what respect means to both of you and how you can better show it. If you feel like your partner isn't respecting you, then try to give specific reasons or details as an example.

They say that honesty is the best policy, and nothing could be closer to the truth when it comes to relationships where one partner is away. If you aren't honest then the other person will pick up on this. This can lead to breakdowns in communication and trust issues. It might not seem like such a big thing at the time, but if your partner begins to doubt you, then they begin to doubt other things that you say or do in the relationship.

Make sure that you always let your partner know that you love them, and how you're feeling. If you're missing them, then just let them know this. You don't have to try to make them feel bad for being away, but often just knowing that they're still being missed and you care about them can be a good boost. It may seem like it will upset them and it could, but making them feel like you don't even care is worse. Talking over the phone and expressing your feelings can prove hard for some people, but there are other ways. You could write them a letter or an email and tell them how you feel that way.

It isn't always just about the other person who is away either. If you're running around and staying out late, that won't be positive for your relationship. It could be innocent, but if it's mistaken by the other person, then it could be hazardous for your relationship. Just take some time and try to think about how your actions could be affecting the other person in the relationship.

Keeping up communication with your partner while you're away, or they're away, is very important. We have covered some great ways to do this in another chapter, so we won't go into the different ways here. What we will try to cover is what to communicate. It may seem trivial to you at the time, but to someone who is away from their family and friends, it's the little things that make all the difference.

- Share as much as you can about what you get up to during your day, just like you would if your partner was at home with you. Make sure that you're honest and let them know that you miss them, but be positive. Tell them that you're managing well and miss them, but you will be okay until they're home again.

- If problems or situations do arise, make sure that you let your partner know. Discuss options with them and make sure that you follow through with decisions that are made. Tell them how the situation was resolved and where things stand. This will let your partner know that they're still involved and make them feel connected with things that are happening while they're away.

- Always try to speak as clearly as possible during your correspondence. You have to remember that the time between conversations could be days, which may leave the other person confused and possibly anxious. If you don't understand something, then make sure that you clarify it until you're both satisfied that you understand exactly what's happening.

- Things will be different when the other person returns home. This doesn't change if they were away a year or a few weeks. People's roles change, and you have to be understanding of this. Just like the roles change, so do the people. Make sure that you talk about the changes and be honest with each other about them. It all comes back to good, honest lines of communication. It's healthy and helpful to talk about things as much as possible.

- Send presents and care packages to your loved one while they are away. Include any personal correspondence from you or the children. This can be quite helpful for the person is away; it allows them to remember the good things and what they have to look forward to when they return home to friends, family and loved ones.

Just remember that at times communication isn't always easy or practical. Your partner could be deployed on tasks or maybe they work long shifts. Communications aren't always guaranteed, so try to be patient and don't take it out on the other person if it is something that is out of their control.

Long-distance relationships can be hard, especially on new couples or newlyweds. Just try to be as patient as possible with one another, be realistic and work on any problems as they arise. Don't let them fester, as they won't go away or improve magically all by themselves. There are always going to be hard times in any relationship, especially new ones, and when you combine that with long distances it can be extremely hard. Don't panic too much if you have fights, just remember to communicate how you're feeling and try to resolve issues as they arrive.

If you know someone who has dealt with issues like this before, reach out and talk to them about how you're feeling and how they dealt with their particular issues. If there are people around you who have partners that are in the military or their partners are working away from home, they will be able to provide you with valuable information. Compromise is a key ingredient to any discussion. It is okay to reach a compromise if it is better for the relationship.

It isn't all doom and gloom either. Separations can give partners the chance to grow and mature, in ways that they might not have had with their partner around.

If things feel like they are getting out of control, don't be a martyr. There are always professionals available who will be able to offer you valuable help. If it's in the military, they have excellent support groups for partners of members that are deployed. If your partner is working in a FIFO position you may have to seek professional help from a private party. Don't let things escalate to the point where there is no hope of turning back.

Chapter Four

IS IT TIME TO MAKE THE NEXT STEP? MEETING FOR THE FIRST TIME

Part One

Safety First

I F YOU HAVE been having a long-distance relationship with someone but have never met them before, it's always important to pay special attention to safety. These days, with people being able to meet online, they aren't always who they portray themselves to be. This could be a slight exaggeration of their looks, all the way through to being totally dishonest about who they really are. There are a lot of people out there who are not well mentally, but there are certain ways in which you can improve your safety.

Remember, just because you think you know someone, you don't always. It always pays to take as many precautions as possible to guarantee your safety. You might only get one chance to do it right; life doesn't give us a lot of second chances. It pays to treat every meeting for the first time like this, whether it's a long-distance friend or perhaps a blind date.

When you meet for the first time, always make sure that the first meeting is in a public place. Often people can be great over the phone, or their photographs look amazing, but in person it's quite the opposite. We quite often get a feeling about a person after we meet them that you just can't get over the phone or through correspondence. If you're in a public place you have more people around in case you get a bad feeling about the other person. It isn't just a precaution if they're creepy or dishonest either. Often it can be more relaxing to meet in a public place where there is less pressure.

Remember that old saying that if anything can go wrong, it will, so always be prepared. Arrange somewhere for you to stay. You have to make sure that you're the one who is in control of the situation, as that way you will have somewhere to go if things don't go the way that you like. You won't feel pressured to stay somewhere if things don't feel right. If your perfect guy turns out to be not so perfect you'll have somewhere to stay away from them where you'll be safe.

Try not to plan on staying months somewhere if you're meeting for the first time. You don't want to be stuck with no way of returning home unless you pay costly cancellation fees. It is easy to extend a stay if things go really well, and it won't cost you as much money. Or you could plan on a return trip for a longer period if they're your dream partner. Before you leave make sure that you let friends and family know where you're going. The more people who know what's happening, and where and when, the better it will be for someone to know if you don't check in for a few days.

You have to be prepared, just like that old saying! If you're flying, allow for missed flights, delayed flights, overbooked flights etc. Pack a change of clothes in your carry-on bag in case the airline loses all of yours. Have some cash ready in case of an emergency where you may need to book alternate accommodation. Quite often you will have to arrange your own place to stay and then try to chase people later to get reimbursed. If you're driving, get your car serviced, make sure your battery is charged and your spare tire is ready to go. Make sure that your cell phone is fully charged, you have credit on it and you have your charging cable. Try to write down people's numbers on a piece of paper and put them in your wallet or purse. This way, if your phone or laptop dies, you have a hard copy available. The more prepared you are, the smoother things will go. It's always safer to be ready than having to try to deal with things on the fly.

Don't be afraid to walk away if things aren't going as well as you thought. Remember, it won't always be love at first sight, but if you get a bad feeling about someone it pays to pay attention to that feeling. Don't run away and not say anything either, as they might worry about where you've gone. Send them a message or call them. Same for your friends and family, let them know that things didn't work out and you're on the way home.

Remember, don't let all the excitement get too much for you! Make sure that leading up to your first visit you take care of yourself. Eat well and make sure you keep up any exercise, but don't overdo it. You don't want to be sick or exhausted for that first meeting; you may need all your strength! Rest well and eat well.

Don't be afraid to bring them something as a small gift. Everyone loves presents, right? It doesn't have to be very expensive, just something small to let them know that you've thought of them. Guys, if you've met a girl, maybe it could just be something small like a bunch of flowers. (Ben did this when he met me at the airport!) It can also be an excellent way to break the tension and give you something small to get the conversation started. Relax and just be yourself, it's not much good pretending to be something that you're not. If they don't like you for who you are, it's never going to work out.

Try and plan events and activities where you can both relax for that first day. Don't put a lot of pressure on yourselves to do all of the work.

Even though you probably both know each other extremely well, those first few hours together can be full of nerves and awkwardness, so don't try to push it too hard.

Now that you have made all of this effort, sit back and enjoy your time together. This is a special time between the two of you that you will never be able to replicate again, so treat every minute as if it is precious. Enjoy each other - you deserve to be happy!

Part Two
When Should You Meet For The First Time?

So you have been talking to someone online or perhaps through more traditional ways, such as mail or phone calls, and things are going great. What next? When is it time to meet for the first time? This could be the best thing that ever happened, or it could be just a one-off, you never know. We are going to give you some ideas below of signs to look for, to let you know that it's time to meet. If you find yourself spending more time talking to this person than any other, or perhaps every five minutes you are checking to see if they have messaged, it could be time to take that next big step!

When you're chatting with people online or via text and they always message you straight back, then perhaps they are into you as much as you're into them. It's a good sign to look for! If there seems to be big gaps between conversations or you're always the one who initiates the conversation then maybe they aren't as keen as you think they are. People who are consistent in their conversation show that they are engaged with it, they are interested in it and in the person that they are having it with. If they are giving you priority, then they obviously care about you somewhat. If they forget to write you back or it seems like they don't have enough time for you, maybe they aren't that interested. You have to look at this in a practical way and try not to blow it out of proportion. If you care about someone or love someone, then you will go out of your way to prioritize them in your life.

Sometimes you just know that someone is right for you. Whether or not they feel the same way is harder to work out. If they have already expressed their feelings and you have similar feelings to them, then go with your gut instinct. Often our first impressions and gut instincts of the people are quite on the money. It doesn't pay to ignore it if your head is screaming "I think they're the one" right from the beginning, especially if you both feel the same way about each other.

If you find yourself just messaging back and forth about the small things that happen to you both during the day. Maybe you both have the need to tell each other all the small things, about what happened at work or just a funny story on the drive home. If you're just as happy to read their messages as they are to read yours, then these are all great signs. Most of life is made up of all these small things, day-to-day happenings that you share with a loved one. This could be the person that you would be happy to come home to after a hard day's work or the person with whom you would rather spend all of your waking time with.

If you both have similar ideas on timing, when your relationship should progress, dating, marriage or first meetings, then obviously you have some things in common. It can mean nothing or it could mean everything. Sam and I had different ideas on our timelines, but we still worked it out and managed to get together. If two people can be happy while alone, it shows that they will be stronger when they are together. It also tells you that they won't be needy and constantly seek attention if you have to be separated for short periods of time.

If you can share bad experiences with someone who you enjoy spending time with, they should be able to listen to well and help you deal with them. When you find yourselves sitting back and laughing and joking about the bad things with someone it shows that you can open up with each other. You want to spend your life with someone who is able to go with the bad times, just as well as they go with the good times. It isn't always easy to find someone who you can share everything with. You need to reach out and grab hold of those people in your life; surround yourself with them. You don't need people who are only around for the good times, but disappear during the bad times, when you need them the most.

If your online relationship begins to feel like a normal relationship, then maybe it's time to take that next step. Sam and I try to continue our relationship as much as possible when apart, we often just go about our day-to-day lives with each other in our ears. We talk and watch shows together, play games online together, and sometimes we just work and chat. That's when you know it's time to take the next step, when you feel like you have known someone your entire life.

CHAPTER FIVE

TELLING FRIENDS & FAMILY ABOUT YOUR LONG-DISTANCE RELATIONSHIP

ONE OF THE most daunting things that we face during an online or long-distance relationship is how to explain it to everyone. You have friends and family that all want to know everything that's going on, who you're dating and talking to all the time. It can be a delicate conversation; some people are quite understanding, while others are not so.

When you are in a long-distance relationship you find yourselves talking about things a lot earlier than normal couples would. You talk about things like children, living together, moving and marriage for example. The reason normal couples don't talk about these things so early is because there just isn't the need for it. There is no rush and no long-term planning required for two people who are dating in the same city. They don't have children, ex-partners or immigration to worry about, so you don't have to think years into the future. People that are involved in a long-distance relationship will often find themselves in a unique situation where their friends and family have no practical advice to offer.

So how do you explain to everyone that you have fallen in love with a complete stranger that you've never met? Well, not so easily, but it isn't impossible. We will try to explain some ideas and advice to help you have that one-in-a-million conversation.

Speaking from personal experience here, I told my mum and dad, and they were quite understanding. They aren't that old and didn't think it was too crazy, although my mum thought that Sam may kill me and rob me the first time we met! Yeah, a girl travels all the way around the world to kill a strange man; not really that likely. Sam told her mother, who was really supportive. Side note here, Sam had previously had a pen pal that she had traveled to the United Kingdom to meet when she was younger, and had also traveled around Europe.

Before you tell everyone about your blossoming romance you have to remember that everyone will react differently to the news; no two people are exactly the same. Some may be really supportive, others think you're both crazy, and some people may be completely against the idea. These are all different reactions that have to be handled as they happen. You will have to tailor each approach differently, depending on how you think the person may react to your news.

You don't have to run around and tell everyone what is happening in your life. Depending on your situation you may not have to tell any-one about it specifically. One of the easiest ways to tell people about it is as they ask; let the conversation come about naturally. You don't have to push it, and the more natural it seems, the easier it will be for people to accept it. Your close friends and family will find out first, depending on how close you are to them. The closer your friends are, the sooner it will come up in conversation. Don't feel like you have to tell anyone if you don't want to. Ultimately, it will be your decision when and where you let people know.

You could choose to bring the conversation up yourself and sit your friends or family down and explain your situation to them. The only problem with this is that it will come across as you simply telling them, instead of them asking about what's happening. They may not be as interested as you think, and it may force their reaction to be somewhat artificial compared to the conversation coming up naturally. Try to time the conversation as well as you can; you don't want to spring it all on people at a critical time. Wait until it's a casual situation, over dinner or relaxing, and give people the chance to absorb the information.

If all of that fails then you will be left with the last resort, so to speak. Wait until your plans are in motion and then spring it on everyone. This is probably one of the least favorable ways of going about it, as not many people like surprises like this! By letting your friends and family know about your relationship and plans you are including them, making them feel as if they are a part of your life and future. If you wait until your plans are already in motion, you are telling them that you don't really care about or value their opinions. The only real reason for doing it this way was if the people who you were telling wouldn't approve of your decisions. Think about it - if they wouldn't approve or throw judgments around, are they really worth being friends with in the first place? A family that doesn't approve are another kettle of fish altogether. They will either come around or they won't; after all, we don't choose our family.

Just try to remember that ultimately, it's about you and your happiness. If you are both happy, and happy with the way things are going, then it's up to you. We can't make everyone happy all the time; it's impossible and you would go crazy trying. The best we can do is make ourselves happy, and try to be as understanding to those around us as possible.

Most of the time the people who don't approve will have certain reasons for their concerns. They genuinely aren't concerned for no reason and you can only do your best to address these concerns. If you know what some of their questions will be, you'll be better prepared to answer them.

First of all, they will be concerned with losing contact with you.

You may be in another state or another country, and they will be worried that they won't be able to see you as much as they like, or talk to you as often as before. Try to reassure them that there are heaps of different ways that you'll be able to stay in touch, like we discussed in the communication chapter. You won't be able to see them every day, but there is still email, messages, letters or video chats. Try to remind them that even though you may be further apart you will still be friends and you still need them to be a part of your life.

They might be worried that after you travel all this distance to be with your partner, if anything was to happen you wouldn't be able to get back home. They could also be worried that you may change your mind and want to return back home, but not be able to do so. It can be a hard question to answer, but you have to do your best to remind them that you're the one who is in the long-distance relationship, and ultimately it's up to you what you decide to do. Let them know that you have an amazing group of friends and family that you can rely on if things did happen to change.

Another common question from friends and family will be "Have you thought this through?" At first you might be tempted to say, "Well of course we have," but try to think of it from their point of view. They are only concerned about you after all. This is a good opportunity to tell them exactly how much you have thought it through, the research that you have done and how ready you both are.

If you have gone through all of this and you're ready to make that big step, then good luck to you. The important thing to remember is to take your time, and be as patient as possible. Nothing will happen overnight, especially if immigration is involved, so try not to let any delays get you down. Both people involved in the long-distance relationship have a lot of work to do, and many sacrifices to make. Good luck to you in your future life. We wish you all the happiness that we both have.

CHAPTER SIX
MAKING IT A VISIT TO REMEMBER

IF YOU'RE CURRENTLY in a long-distance relationship, then you know that those visits can be the most exciting and heartbreaking times of your life. There are never enough visits, so you want to get the most out of them while you can. If money is an issue, try not to overspend on the visit. Sam and I often find that some of the most memorable times that we have are when we just hang out together, like a normal couple. Sure, hotels, flights, getaways and touring are all amazing, but sitting on the couch cuddled up together watching television is special. That's the time that we miss most when we are apart from each other, the normal couple things we do together. Things like cooking a meal or just going for a walk with the dogs to the park are what you need to do, just like a normal couple would. You don't have to be doing something every minute of the day; just hang out, relax and enjoy each other's touch. Sam and I love going to the movies, waiting until certain movies are out, then just spending a couple of hours holding hands and eating popcorn. It isn't anything extravagant, just a couple of quiet hours watching a great movie, enjoying being with each other.

You want every visit to be as memorable as possible, as these are the memories that will get you through until you see each other again. We like to take a lot of photos of each other. Some of them are serious, Sam makes me retake them until she's happy, while others are just silly dumb photos. Either way, this gives us something to look back on and remember the great times that we had during our visit.

The visits are fantastic, the arrival amazing, but the farewell makes you feel like you're being torn apart from the inside out. No matter how many times we have done it, it never gets any easier. If it was easy to say goodbye for days, weeks or months, then it wouldn't be worth all the problems.

That first moment when you see your soulmate walking through the airport, or getting out of a car, nothing can describe how excited you are. It starts off days before, getting more and more nervous and excited. Then it turns into hours before they arrive; often it feels just like it did the very first time that you met them. The kisses, the hugs, holding hands, their smell, their taste. All of it is just so damn good; words alone aren't good enough to describe how happy you are, especially if it's been months.

We will try to cover a few ideas that you could use to make your visits even more special. Remember, it's the visits that are the reward for the separation. They are your present for all that time apart! You need to make the most of them, and get as much of the things that you normally miss out on!

You could consider a surprise visit. Obviously this is easier for some rather than others. It might not be practical for their or your work situations. I can hardly fly to another country when it takes approximately 30-40 hours traveling time without raising a few suspicions. The longest that we have ever spent without talking is when one of us is stuck on an international flight, and can't call or message. You don't have to randomly show up to make it a surprise either. Perhaps you could tell your partner that you'll be arriving during a certain week, but not exactly when. That way they'll be even more excited and nervous, not knowing when you could walk up and kiss them or surprise them during their day.

If you plan and pay for certain activities beforehand it will give you a better handle on your finances and what your plans will be. You can book and pay for flights, hotels, coupons, movie tickets, meals or even a car rental. This gets a few different things accomplished. First, you know what some of your plans will be, and how long you have for anything else that might come up. Secondly, it gives you things to get excited about together; you can look for hotels, flights, events and even restaurants together. Talking about and planning these activities seems to help when you're separated for long periods of time. Having something exciting to look forward to can be a great help if you're both feeling a bit down, or upset about the separation. Even if you can't afford to do a lot of things, keep a shared list together. Add to the list or cross things off when you finally get them accomplished, as the more that you do together, the happier you both will be.

We can't ignore the physical aspect of those long-awaited visits either. We won't go into it too much in this section as we plan on devoting an entire section to it! Don't be scared to put extra effort in when it comes to sexytime; you have both been waiting a long time, so make sure it's special! Maybe you could consider booking a hotel or motel room for that first night. It doesn't have to be five stars either, just somewhere you don't have to worry about parents, friends or flatmates.

Don't be scared to meet your partner with flowers or another thoughtful present. It doesn't have to be expensive, just make sure that you put a little extra effort in. A bunch of flowers could be something that she saves for a very long time! Pay attention to what your partner likes and what they've been missing while you're apart. If he likes a certain perfume, then try to wear it on the day. I personally will never forget what Sam smelt like after she walked out of customs at the airport, and what she tasted like, ha ha. She has a certain sort of fruity body spray that she likes, and always seems to pick the same chewing gum.

Whenever she is chewing that gum it always makes me remember that very first meeting.

Remember to spend as much time together as possible. You're probably thinking, well duh, and I know that Sam and I are basically inseparable while we are together. The longest we went on a four-week visit was 2.5 hours away, once. You could take time off work, or arrange to swap shifts with other people if possible. It won't be possible to take months off work, but even a few extra days can make all the difference.

It's the normal things that you miss whilst you're both apart. Things like going to sleep together, waking up together, or just sitting on a couch holding hands or laying down cuddled up watching a television show or movie. If you can put off going to the local bar with your friends after work, do it. Better yet, you could take her or him and hang out with your friends together. Don't spend the whole visit doing it though. Your friends will understand that during your visits it's your time to be together as much as possible.

CHAPTER SEVEN
HOW TO DEAL WITH PROBLEMS WHILST IN A LONG-DISTANCE RELATIONSHIP

I T DOESN'T MATTER what sort of relationship you find yourself in, there will always be fights. That's something that is pretty much guaranteed in life - when a boy and a girl, or two boys, or two girls get together they will fight. Two people in a relationship that don't fight will one day just explode; that's when you hear about people beating their partners. They hold in all the little things until they build up, then they let them all out and they explode. If something comes up in your relationship, sometimes it's healthy to just have a fight, and get it over and dealt with. There is a flip side to that also; if you're both fighting like two cats in a bag there might just be some other issues altogether.

When you're in a long-distance relationship the fights take on another aspect altogether. Sam and I don't often fight when we are both together; every now and again we'll have a small fight, but not often. We do fight when we are apart, not all the time, but still there is the odd fight. When someone is 10,000 miles away, it isn't easy to have a fight, then kiss and make up. We are both pretty stubborn too, which doesn't help. Both of us have developed certain ways in which we fight also, both quite the opposite to each other. I like to just ignore a fight; after a while I'm happy to just move on and forget that it ever happened. Sam on the other hand likes to get right into it; she doesn't want to sleep or move on until the issue has been dealt with. So, two different fighting techniques, thousands of miles apart, it sometimes makes it pretty hard to just kiss, make up, and then move on.

It probably doesn't help that we have both had previous relationships where we have had to deal with this sort of thing constantly. It's hard to not bring in your emotional baggage from a previous relationship, but it definitely won't help your new one. When two people have a fight in a normal relationship, it normally follows the same pattern. You have an argument or fight, you kiss and make up, then you move on. There is a certain amount of face-to-face contact that makes it easy to see the emotion in the other person's face. You can instantly tell that they are hurt, disappointed, angry, upset, resentful and when they are sorry. In a long distant relationship you're missing all of those aspects of the fight. You rely on your instincts a lot more; you're looking for signs in the way they write, the way they sound and how long it takes for them to respond.

We have a slight twist on this as well. Because I suffer from depression and anxiety attacks I can't just turn off my phone and cool down for a few hours. Sam would instantly turn from angry and upset to worried and panicked. We normally try to settle any issues before the other has to go to sleep. I for one would have never done that before; I was quite happy to go days and days without speaking to my ex, even though we lived together. This is how Sam likes to handle disagreements, and I find it to be a pretty good idea. You never know what could happen while you're asleep, so it's best to try to just hash out the fight and reach some sort of conclusion. Everyone will be different, there is no cookie-cutter approach to handling fights, let alone in a long distance relationship, so take what you can and always try to do the best you can. Just remember, without the kiss and make up part at the end, fighting is just that much harder on everyone. Hopefully you'll find some of the following advice helpful, and end up living happily ever after.

One of the biggest relationship issues, not just for long-distance relationships, is that old green-eyed monster, jealousy. The number of relationships that this little gremlin has ended alone is crazy; if you wrote them all down in a list, it would probably wrap the entire world up. There is always a little bit of jealousy in any relationship, but when there is too much it will tear that relationship apart. When you're already suffering from a lack of attention in a relationship, thinking that the other person is paying someone else attention can lead to depression and anger. It's a slippery slope once you start sliding down it, and leads to many other problems in a relationship. If you are constantly worried about what your partner is doing, where they are and who they're with, then they will start to resent you for it. Even though they are doing nothing wrong, they might start lying to you about what they're doing, so that they can avoid fights. You have to establish certain boundaries in your relationship, lay down the rules that you are happy with and compromise. Trust, after all, is the foundation of all successful relationships, long distance or not.

It doesn't matter if your partner is a saint - maybe they cure disease and fight fires, then on weekends they do charity work and rescue orphaned animals - they will always have certain habits or things that they do that irritate you. When you're in a long-distance relationship you have to learn how to keep all of these small things in some sort of perspective. Don't blow your lid on a little thing, take some time and just think it through. The fights are that much harder in long-distance relationships, so you have to try your hardest to avoid them. Think about the issue over the period of a year, for example, will it still matter? If it won't then maybe it isn't worth fighting about it now.

You have to fight fairly during a fight, not just in long-distance relationships, but in all relationships in general. The main purpose of fighting is to resolve an issue that is bothering one of you so try to be constructive and actually resolve the issue. Don't just fight for the sake of fighting. Don't turn your phone off and ignore the other person either. When you are miles away from each other this is the only way of staying in contact, so to just turn your phone off and ignore the other person is quite hurtful. If you try to focus on telling each other why you're upset and how the way they are acting is affecting you, then you will be on the right track to sorting out the problem.

Just remember everyone fights, especially about little things that make us frustrated. If you are starting to feel down or depressed, try to think back to when you first met, when you fell in love with them and why you fell in love. Remind yourself why this relationship is so important to you, and think about what it's worth to keep it intact.

CHAPTER EIGHT

OUR TOP 6 THINGS TO DO WHEN APART

THERE ARE A million things to do when you are apart, and these can all be found by a quick Google search. So instead, we decided to tell you only our favorite things.

1. **Face-to-Face Call**

   The reason this is our favorite thing to do is because most of our conversations are just phone calls or texting. So, every weekend we try to FaceTime (we are iOS users). It's funny how much you appreciate these phone calls. Most people can't find time to FaceTime every day, but make sure you do it often as you can. This creates a connection that is sometimes lost without face-to-face communication.

2. **Games**

   For us, games are a huge part of our life. The reason we are Ben & Sam is because of a game. We enjoy playing many games together, but we usually mix it up between games on our phones to PlayStation games. Even if you have never been a fan of games, I would suggest trying it out. Also, the biggest thing here for us is that we always have our headsets in while we play. This way you get the same effect of playing beside each other and you can still carry on a conversation.

3. **Gifts**

When we first started, we mailed each other things. I know - how old school of us, but honestly I miss this part of it only because I loved getting the package in the mail. The first package I ever sent him was a birthday gift for him. I was so nervous sending it to him, as we were only friends at that point, but it was still a big step for us as we gave out our addresses to each other. I remember the first birthday card he sent me, I got to see his handwriting for the first time. Weird how something so small could mean so much to me! It made him more real; this was before we had met. My favorite gift from him was his favorite T-shirt which I still wear to bed sometimes. So take the time to sneak some gifts in. Depending on whether or not you are different countries, send things they can't get at home. Also, be sure to include a piece of you.

4. **20 Questions**

This never gets old no matter how long you have been together. When we first got together it was me that came up with these questions. So yes, probably more the woman's approach to things than the man, but I did get him to create his own list a few times. This was a way to explore questions that we had for each other that we hadn't gotten around to answering. As a heads up make you are ready to play truthfully and you are ready for answers. If you are going to answer with lies then you have already started the slippery slope downwards.

5. **Journal**

This is something we don't do often, but when we are both struggling. He has access to my one email, so we share the Notes folder on our iPhones. The first time it happened he was having a rough night; he didn't want to wake me up so he wrote in the notepad. I didn't notice right away, and he asked me if I had seen it. I checked it out and we went from there. It was a place to leave messages that wasn't through texts. A place to explain our feelings.

6. **Plan**

One thing that we seem to be amazing at is planning our next trips to see each other. Time seems to move really slowly when you are separated, but making a plan can help create excitement. Once we have our flight booked, we usually have at least one major thing planned. We have done road trips around Tasmania together to a weekend away to Chicago. Then there are the little things, like new restaurants we both want to try together or movies that are coming out that we can see. Even the smallest plan can make you excited. Use a shared calendar to organize things.

These are just our favorites, and I am sure everyone has their own. The biggest thing for us depends on the length we are apart. If it's 6 weeks we tend to just go with the normal daily routine of our lives. Any longer than that and we delve into different areas as sometimes we run out of things to talk about after a boring day at work.

CHAPTER NINE
IMMIGRATION

Y OU'RE FINALLY THERE; together, you have decided to close
the distance. Congrats, except wait - it's not that easy if you live
in two different countries. As this book is for all LDR couples I will try
to give you broad tips that should help ease some of the stress, but saying that, I am not an immigration specialist so make sure you consult a
professional if you have any questions.

There are many different ways to close the distance with your signif-
icant other. Depending on your age, country and status, you could do
a student visa, working travel visa, work visa, or if you decide to marry
then there is also the option of sponsoring your spouse for residency.
One of the things I want to stress here is that every couple is different.
Therefore, make sure you make decisions that work for both of you.

Working Holiday Visas

One of the best options for the under-30 crowd is a working holiday
visa. This visa will get you into a country and let you work and travel
for a specific amount of time. Each country has its own specifications,
but we found this website that lists all countries with this type of visa and
it gives descriptions to requirements involved. This visa in my opinion

is the easiest visa to use when it comes to trying out a normal relationship with your LDR. There is no long-term commitment and the time involved in getting the visa is relatively short.

Student Visas

This option is always available, but this is an expensive option if education isn't needed or you're on a budget. I went with this option as when we first met I was over 30 and there was no other choice for us at the time. This option also gave us the option to live together for 5 months to decide if this 10,000-mile LDR was worth all the aggravation that came with it. Thankfully, it was! This is an example; the program I took over in Australia was $8500 AUD compared to the same course but 4 months longer over in Canada at $2400 CAD. So, as you can tell, the option to study abroad may seem fascinating but you also need the finances to fund it. Make sure you explore the options.

Working Visa

Depending on your trade or skills, this option won't work. Some countries are looking for skilled workers, but as Ben & I found out that it isn't always that easy. If you are a skilled worker, then I would suggest checking out this option as it's a way to work full time. There are usually two types of working visas - temporary and working class visas. Once again, check with your country's immigration office for requirements.

Permanent Residency Visa

Last but not least, here is the hardest process of all. It might be named differently depending on the country you are looking to move to. This visa is for couples who are legally married or have been living common law or conjugal. Out of all the visas this is the most difficult and the most permanent.

Most of the visas are pretty self-explanatory in nature, but there are some tips that we have learned from our process with the permanent residency application that I thought I would share.

- Make sure you keep all proof of travel to each other's countries. Passports are great, just make sure that you keep old ones for the future.

- Pictures - doesn't seem like a hard thing, but in ours they wanted to see proof of everything, from start of our relationship to our wedding. So make sure you take pictures from start to present.

- When you visit each other's countries, make sure that you introduce your SO to each other's family and friends. They ask this question on your application with times and dates.

- Tip: Like a lot of people we are both on Facebook; one thing we didn't realize we were doing was that when we did check in's and status updates we were making a time-stamped diary of our time together.

- If you run into a snag, Google it for an answer... but if you can't find an actual reliable source I suggest getting a consult with an immigration lawyer. We came across a few issues that I just couldn't find the answer to, and since we didn't want delays we found a local immigration lawyer that does consults for cheap. We got our answers without having to spend big.

All said and done it's an exhausting experience for both of you. Make sure you are both prepared for the process as it will take effort, and if you aren't ready it could divide you.

Chapter Ten
YOUR LONG DISTANCE STORIES

Couple 1

Your Names:

Mariah L and Elizabeth S

Ages:

29 and 27

Where are you both from?

Mariah is from Colorado, USA and I, Elizabeth, am from Alaska, USA.

Have you met in person yet?

Yes, we have met several times over the last year. Travelling is difficult for both of us, as we have very committed careers that are demanding. Mariah is a national parks ranger in Colorado, and I'm a marine biologist.

How did you meet?

We met through an animal conservationist forum that we were both members of. We had been friends for some time on the forum before we started to talk more socially off the website.

How do you handle being apart?

It isn't easy. It's harder on Mariah, as she is surrounded by many people and constantly seeing happy couples together. I live in a remote part of Alaska, where I'm studying and working, and being alone is part of my career.

Do you have a closing the distance date? Who will be moving where?

At this point, we are still several years away from being able to permanently make the move, but a date is penciled in. Once my research position is finished, I'll be eligible to look for another position.

Worst part of being in a LDR?

The distance! We both miss cuddling on cold nights and simply enjoying each other's company. It would be nice up here in Alaska on a cold night to come home from being out in the field to spend time with Mariah.

Best part of being in a LDR?

The personal information and feelings we share. When we spend time together on the phone or video chatting, we have each other's attention 100% of the time. I think it has brought us much closer together than many traditional relationships.

Do you have a funny LDR moment?

No, not really. The first time we met each other's parents was interesting, but both families are very supportive.

Do you have a sad LDR moment?

Every time we have to say goodbye to each other is a sad moment.

One piece of advice for other couples involved in an LDR or thinking of starting one?

It's hard work, but if you're happy to do the hard work, then the good times are worth it.

Couple 2

Your Names:

Ian & Leilani

Ages:

28 & 26

Where are you both from?

Baltimore, Maryland & Honolulu, Hawaii

Have you met in person yet?

Yes

How long have you been together?

We have been together for 2.5 years.

How did you meet?

Ian: I was in Hawaii for some training, as I am a Marine. A group of us went out for dinner on our night off, and she was our waitress. As soon as she smiled, I knew I needed to talk to her. We were a bunch of rowdy marines, which didn't help her first impression. A few times I caught her eyes and received such a sweet smile. My friends weren't helping me, so as we were leaving, I pretended I left my wallet on the table and I ran back in. She was just passing by when I said hi. She seemed so shy but say hi back. I asked her if she wanted to meet for coffee tomorrow if she was off. Then I mumbled, unless you are with someone. She laughed and said no. She then looked me right in the eye and said yes. She told me she would meet me the next day at the little restaurant down the round. The rest is history.

Leilani: When Ian walked in with his friends, I noticed him right away. The rest of them were rowdier than he was. He had the cutest smile with dimples. Yes, I was looking the whole time I was trying to serve him. I thought little of it until he ran back in. But when he asked me out, I knew I had to take a chance, so I said yes.

How do you handle being apart?

We can't say we are used to it, but it is what it is. Ian loves being a marine, and I support him in this. We make sure when we get time together we spend every moment together and make sure we spend normal couple time with our family and friends. When he's away, we try to make sure we communicate as much as possible. Video calls are less often, as it depends on where he is, but those are the moments we look forward to. The rest of the time, we email each other. At the end of each day, we send an email letting the other know what they have done. Sometimes, it's boring, but I would rather have that contact than nothing.

Do you have a closing the distance date? Who will be moving where?

We closed the distance in the sense that Leilani moved to Virginia, where I am based right now. She's finishing her nursing degree. Unfortunately, we still live apart often when I get deployed or go away to training. So far, we haven't had to spend longer than 6 months apart. But I appreciate that she was willing to pick up her life and move to Virginia for me. We just got engaged and plan to marry in Spring 2018.

Worst part of being in a LDR?

Ian: I miss the contact with her. When we are together, we try to spend as much time together as possible, so it's like being ripped apart every time I leave.

Leilani: Being away from my family and friends makes it harder when Ian is away. At the start, I was lonely, which put pressure on us, as I was constantly upset. But since I started back at school, I have met friends, and his family has taken me in as one of their own, which has helped.

Best part of being in a LDR?

The first touch after being apart for a long time

Do you have a funny LDR moment?

This might be inappropriate, but we got caught in an intimate moment while he was deployed. We had been doing a video chat, and we weren't doing anything horrible, but I was teasing with my shirt and bra when his bunkmate walked in; because of the size of the screen, he saw more than I would have liked. I just looked, and I saw his friend with his mouth open standing behind him. I screamed and laughed and ran from the screen. Ian was mortified, as was I. They made jokes for weeks about it with him. Ian's response was, you wish you had what I had haha. I have since met him, and he apologized profusely for walking in, and he's a great friend.

Do you have a sad LDR moment?

We almost broke up when Ian left for the first time. We were about 4 months in, and where he was, he couldn't communicate with me as much as I needed. I say I needed only because I was suffering from some depression. I had only been in Virginia for about 2 months before he got deployed, so I didn't get to settle before he left. Thankfully, we made it through, but it was touch and go for a few weeks.

One piece of advice for other couples involved in an LDR or thinking of starting one?

Be 100% in it. A LDR will never work unless both parties are totally in it. You know your heart better than anyone else, so make decisions based on you, not everyone's else's opinions, as people will have them.

Couple 3

Your Names:

Giovanni & Ai

Ages:

22 & 21

Where are you both from?

Italy & China

Have you met in person yet?

Yes

How long have you been together?

We became friends in 2015 and together as partners in 2016.

How did you meet?

We met online in a backpackers' forum. Giovanni was planning a trip with his friends to China, and I noticed his questions were things I knew, so I replied to the thread. We continued to go back and forth until we finally exchanged emails. We did this for months. We knew what the other person looked like, but we had never done a video chat or even a phone call. Ironically, I was away on holidays with my family when he came to visit. After 6 months, we had our first phone call and it lasted hours. We didn't run out of things to talk about. We both enjoy photography, so we talked about all the places we wanted to go. I don't think either of us had any romantic feelings. He had a girlfriend when we first met, and I didn't see in him in that way. I knew he was one of my closest friends, and I would eventually love to meet up with him. It wasn't until a year later that we found our chance. I had planned a trip to France with my cousin and best friend. He would meet up with us for a few days. We were excited to meet finally, and we had our days planned with things to do together. Just before he left, he and his girl-friend had split up; she was leaving for school abroad. I saw nothing odd about that, but looking back, there were signs he was falling for me. The day we met was sunny, and I was supposed to meet him in front of Arc du Triomphe at noon. I got there early. I was nervous and couldn't understand why, but again, I was ignoring signs. But when you haven't met someone in person, how can you have feelings for them, right? Wrong. I had just looked down for a second, and I looked up and he was walking up to me. He was gorgeous. I had never thought that before. I knew he was a nice-looking guy, but in person, he took my breath away. He was smiling at me and he said, "Mi hai Cambiato la vita." I didn't know what he meant. I am fluent in English but not Italian not. He smiled and leaned in and kissed both of my cheeks. I knew I was blushing, and I said it was so nice to meet him. From there, things changed; as we walked, he held my hand, but he did it like he was helping me through a crowd. But I got butterflies every time he touched me. At the end of the day, we were sitting on a bench outside of my hotel, talking. I asked him what he said earlier, and he said, you have changed my life. I am sure my mouth dropped; it was beautiful. I knew right then I was in love with this man who was my best friend but also the love of my life. I know it sounds corny, but it was beautiful. He extended his trip, and the four of us hung out like we had known each other for years. My cousin and best friend loved him and had no issues with him tagging along. The final day we were at the airport, he couldn't come any further as we were in different parts of the airport. Saying goodbye almost killed us. I was bawling as he walked away. We promised to speak as soon as we could. We have now been together for over a year, and both of our families are supportive. Mine were a little harder to get to come around, but thankfully, my older sister led the way from the traditional customs, so they were not as surprised when I told them I had fallen in love with an Italian. He is working on a work-ing visa to come over and work.

How do you handle being apart?

Same as before, we text and call constantly, and we facetime at least 2-3 nights a week. We just keep involved in each other's lives.

Do you have a closing the distance date? Who will be moving where?

We will know early 2018 if it's been approved. If not, we will try to do it the other way, but my parents want to have him here, before I leave the country.

Worst part of being in a LDR?

We both hate that we miss so many things in each other's lives. Normal events are hard enough, but we have missed birthdays, and I missed his graduation from University, which was hard.

Best part of being in a LDR?

Being in such a strong relationship with someone who lives in another country is something to be proud of. We are so much stronger than a lot of normal couples. We appreciate everything, as we know time is limited for us when we get to see each other.

Do you have a funny LDR moment?

This might be inappropriate, but we got caught in an intimate moment while he was deployed. We had been doing a video chat, and we weren't doing anything horrible, but I was doing teasing with my shirt and bra when his bunkmate walked in; because of the size of the screen, he saw more than I would have liked. I just looked, and I saw his friend with his mouth open standing behind him. I screamed and laughed and ran from the screen. Ian was mortified, as was I. They made jokes for weeks about it with him. Ian's response was, you wish you had what I had haha. I have since met him, and he apologized profusely for walking in, and he's a great friend.

Do you have a sad LDR moment?

Leaving on the plane the first time we met.

One piece of advice for other couples involved in an LDR or thinking of starting one?

If they are worth it, it will happen. Things happen for a reason. I never went into this with the intention of falling in love, especially with some-one from another country, but I did. I love it, and I would not trade it for anything in the world.

CONCLUSION

QUITE OFTEN, BEING involved in a long-distance relationship can be the first step towards a normal relationship. Even more often, it can be the end to a relationship before it even begins. It's definitely not for the faint of heart that's for sure!

We appreciate you taking the time to download and read our book on long-distance relationships, and hope that the information is helpful to you. Every relationship faces bumps in the road, and sometimes, like in long-distance relationships, the bumps may feel more like mountains. Don't let the little bumps destroy what could possibly turn out to be one of the best things that has ever happened to you.

Sam and I would like to hear any of your long-distance relationship stories too. We were hoping to include some in this book, but time limits prevented it from happening. If you want to send your stories to us and have them published in our next book, please email them to bennsamauthor@gmail.com. You can choose to have them published under your own name or we rename them for you. Don't worry about your spelling or grammar either, as we will fix any mistakes for you.

So, thanks again from Sam and myself. We would greatly appreciate any feedback and reviews and thank you in advance for your time.

Ben & Sam

RESOURCES

http://www.oxforddictionaries.com/definition/american_english/
long-distance-relationship

http://www.freemake.com/blog/
best-chat-apps-for-iphone-for-round-the-clock-talking/

http://phandroid.com/2015/02/19/how-to-facetime-on-android-alternatives/

http://www.militaryonesource.mil/health-wellness/
deployment?content_id=268646

http://www.ldrmagazine.com/blog/2014/01/21/
safety-first-tips-follow-meeting-first-time/

http://www.yourtango.com/experts/yourtango-experts/
online-dating-bootcamp-day-10-expert

http://lovemybrit.com/friends-and-family/

http://www.long-distance-lover.com/long-distance-relationship-meeting/

http://everydaylife.globalpost.com/tips-fix-problems-long-distance-relation-
ship-32198.html

Made in the USA
Coppell, TX
17 December 2021